STECK-VAUGH

# Comprehension Skills

# MAIN IDEA

## LEVEL
## F

Linda Ward Beech
Tara McCarthy
Donna Townsend

STECK-VAUGHN
C O M P A N Y
A Subsidiary of National Education Corporation

| | |
|---|---|
| *Executive Editor:* | Diane Sharpe |
| *Project Editor:* | Melinda Veatch |
| *Design Coordinator:* | Sharon Golden |
| *Project Design:* | Howard Adkins Communications |
| *Photographs:* | ©COMSTOCK, Inc. / Tom Drill |

ISBN 0-8114-7854-8

8 9 0 VP 01 00 99 98

The main idea is the point a writer or speaker tries to make about a subject. Learning about main ideas helps you decide what is important.

You are in a city. Tall buildings touch the clouds. A wall of people moves down the sidewalk. You may admire one very tall building or see a friend. These smaller parts by themselves do not make the city. It's the sum of the smaller parts that makes it. The city is the main idea. The people and buildings are details that add up to busy city life.

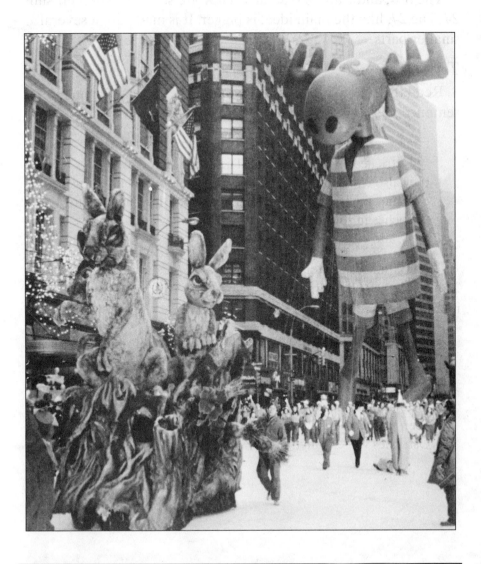

# What Is a Main Idea?

The main idea sentence of a paragraph tells what the paragraph is about. The other sentences are details or small parts. They add up to the main idea. The main idea sentence is often the first or last sentence in a paragraph. But you may find it in the middle of a paragraph, too.

This example may help you think of main ideas:

$$8 \ + \ 9 \ + \ 7 \ = \ 24$$

detail + detail + detail = main idea

The 8, 9, and 7 are like details. They are smaller than their sum, 24. The 24, like the main idea, is bigger. It is made up of several smaller parts.

## Try It!

Read the following story. Then underline the main idea sentence.

◆

Ostriches will eat anything. These birds eat grass, but they also eat wood, stones, bones, and gold. In South Africa, ostriches are hunted for the diamonds that they may swallow. Ostriches in zoos have been known to eat wallets, watches, keys, and coins.

The main idea sentence is the first sentence about ostriches. The other sentences are details. They give examples of what the main idea sentence states.

The main idea could come at the end of the paragraph:

Ostriches eat grass, but they also eat wood, stones, bones, and gold. In South Africa, ostriches are hunted for the diamonds they may swallow. Ostriches in zoos have been known to eat wallets, watches, keys, and coins. Ostriches will eat anything.

# Using What You Know

The main idea is often someone's opinion, not a fact. A writer uses details to convince a reader that his or her opinion is the correct one.

Read the main ideas on this page. Each main idea is an opinion. Write some detail sentences that support the main idea. The first one is done for you.

*Main Idea*: Running is the best exercise.

*Detail*: It strengthens your heart.

*Detail*: It's fun to run with your friends.

*Detail*: It helps you keep fit.

*Main Idea*: My best friend and I are very much alike.

*Detail*: _____

*Detail*: _____

*Detail*: _____

*Main Idea*: My favorite food is _____ .

*Detail*: _____

*Detail*: _____

*Detail*: _____

*Main Idea*: The best movie I've ever seen was _____ .

*Detail*: _____

*Detail*: _____

*Detail*: _____

*Main Idea*: My favorite musical group is _____ .

*Detail*: _____

*Detail*: _____

*Detail*: _____

# Practice Finding the Main Idea

This book asks you to find the main ideas of paragraphs. For example, read the paragraph and answer the question below.

◆

The people of ancient Egypt created an advanced civilization. More than 6,000 years ago, they developed a calendar with 360 days divided into 12 months. The people made paper and learned to write. They built huge monuments with machines they invented.

_B_ **1.** The story mainly tells

    **A.** how people made paper

    **B.** about the creation of Egyptian civilization

    **C.** where an ancient calendar was invented

    **D.** how the people built monuments

The correct answer is **B**. The first sentence says, "The people of ancient Egypt created an advanced civilization." This is the main idea sentence. It tells what the people did. The other sentences are details. They tell how the Egyptians were an advanced society.

Sometimes a story does not have a main idea sentence. It is made up only of details. You put all the details together to find the main idea. Read the story below and answer the question. Write the letter of your answer in the blank.

◆

Microchips provide the power for wristwatches. They are also the brains in our computers, and they control robots. These chips are used in video games and space shuttles. They make our cameras, radios, and televisions small and light.

    **2.** The story mainly tells

    **A.** how computers work

    **B.** why televisions are small

    **C.** how microchips are used

    **D.** how cameras are made

**To check your answer, turn to page 62.**

# How to Use This Book

This book has 25 units with 5 stories in each unit. The stories in units 1 through 12 have main idea sentences. But in units 13 through 25, the stories do not have main idea sentences. Read each story and answer each question. Write the letter of the correct answer in each blank.

When you finish, check your answers on pages 59 through 61. Tear out the answer pages. Fold them to the unit you are checking. Write the number of correct answers in the score box. After you finish the units, work through "Think and Apply" on pages 56 through 58.

## Hints for Better Reading
◆ Units 1–12: Read each story. Ask yourself, "Which sentence is the sum of all the other sentences? Which sentence is like the whole city?" That sentence will be the main idea.

◆ Units 13–25: Read each story. Figure out what the details have in common. What is the writer trying to tell you?

## Challenge Yourself
Try this special challenge. Read the stories and answer the questions. If a story has a main idea sentence, write a sentence using other words to restate the main idea. If a story does not have a main idea sentence, write one for it.

**1.** Imagine testing glass by throwing chickens at it! Sometimes fast-moving airplanes fly through flocks of birds. If the birds hit the windshield of a plane, the glass could shatter and cause a crash. Airplane manufacturers have made a chicken cannon that fires rubber chickens at glass windshields. If the windshield doesn't break when the rubber chicken hits it, the designers know that the glass can withstand the force of a real crash.

**2.** The harmless hognose snake is a champion bluffer. When this snake is threatened, it hisses and acts as if it will bite. If you don't run away, the hognose snake "plays dead." It rolls over on its back, wiggling around as if it's in distress. Then it "dies" with its mouth open and tongue hanging out. If you turn it on its stomach, the snake will roll over on its back again.

**3.** Doctors think that wearing red-tinted glasses can relieve sadness. Some people get very moody and sad in the winter. They may be affected by the brief days. Bright lights help some people, but not everyone. The reddish light coming through rose-colored glasses seems to make people feel happy.

**4.** The Marines had a problem in World War II. Orders were sent in code. But the enemy kept learning the code. Nothing could be kept secret. Then someone thought that Navajo soldiers could help the Marines. Since very few other people could speak Navajo, this language was used as a code. No one on the enemy side knew Navajo either, so the messages stayed secret.

**5.** Dogs have been called our best friends, but they are also good helpers. They can be used in many ways. Some dogs hunt, while others guard animals and property. Boxers and German Shepherds are trained to lead blind people. Doctors test some medicines on dogs. A dog named Laika was the first animal in space.

_____ **1.** The story mainly tells
- **A.** why birds can be dangerous to airplanes
- **B.** how a chicken cannon tests glass
- **C.** how big a bird has to be to damage an airplane
- **D.** how the chicken cannon works

_____ **2.** The story mainly tells
- **A.** where the hognose snake is found
- **B.** what things frighten the hognose snake
- **C.** how dangerous the hognose snake is
- **D.** how the hognose snake bluffs

_____ **3.** The story mainly tells
- **A.** why happy people wear rose-colored glasses
- **B.** when some people get sad
- **C.** how short the daylight is in winter
- **D.** how colored glasses may help people feel better

_____ **4.** The story mainly tells
- **A.** how Navajo people kept secrets
- **B.** when the secret code was used
- **C.** how the Marines used Navajo as a code
- **D.** why the original code had to be changed

_____ **5.** The story mainly tells
- **A.** how many types of dogs there are
- **B.** what the name of the space dog was
- **C.** what kind of dogs can lead blind people
- **D.** how dogs are useful

**1.** Tap dancing started in America. It began as folk dancing that had much kicking and stamping. Over time two kinds of dancing developed. In one kind the dancers wore hard shoes and danced very fast. In the other they wore soft shoes and danced slowly and easily. But there wasn't really any *tap* in tap dancing until 1925, when someone put metal pieces on the toes and heels of tap shoes.

**2.** Probably the best-known rodeo cowboy in the world is Larry Mahan. Mahan was the national champion six times before he was thirty. He was good at every event and was so successful that he had his own plane. When he got too old to ride, he didn't stop. He started a rodeo school.

**3.** It takes more than food to make babies grow up to be healthy and happy. If babies are not patted and hugged, they grow more slowly and are less healthy. Also, they will not be as smart or as happy as adults. Many studies show that love is the most important thing in children's lives.

**4.** Trousers are a recent style in the history of fashion. Men wore tights with short, loose pants over them until the early 1800s when the first real pants for men appeared. Until forty years ago, only men could wear long pants. Boys had to wear shorts. It wasn't until boys started wearing long pants that women began to wear them, too.

**5.** When you take a multiple-choice test, do you ever change your answers? Some scientists think that it is a smart thing to do. They found out that most students who change their answers make the right decision and make better scores on their tests.

_____ **1.** The story mainly tells
- **A.** how there are two kinds of tap dancing
- **B.** how tap shoes are made
- **C.** where some folk dances came from
- **D.** how tap dancing developed

_____ **2.** The story mainly tells
- **A.** where to ride bulls and rope calves
- **B.** about the most famous rodeo cowboy in the world
- **C.** how to get rich in the rodeo
- **D.** where to go to rodeo school

_____ **3.** The story mainly tells
- **A.** why good food is important to babies
- **B.** what makes babies grow up
- **C.** that children need love to grow up healthy
- **D.** how to have smart children

_____ **4.** The story mainly tells
- **A.** how people have worn pants over the years
- **B.** when men stopped wearing pantaloons
- **C.** what boys used to wear
- **D.** when women started wearing trousers

_____ **5.** The story mainly tells
- **A.** how to study for tests
- **B.** what scientists think about answers
- **C.** how to score better on a multiple-choice test
- **D.** which answers to change on tests

**1.** Virgil, a poet in ancient Rome, gave his dead pet a fine funeral. He built a fancy tomb, wrote several poems, and asked friends to mourn with him. It cost about one hundred thousand dollars to bury a housefly! Why did he do this? The government was taking rich people's land away, but land with tombs couldn't be taken from the owners. Virgil used the fly's grave to keep his property.

**2.** Puffed cereal is made in an odd way. The grain, which is usually rice or wheat, is put into large cannons that are then plugged at one end. The cannons are pushed into an oven and heated to 550 degrees. After 40 minutes the cannon plugs are pulled, and hot air rushes into the cannons. Moisture in the cereal grains turns to steam, and the grains puff up like popcorn.

**3.** If you play tennis, you may get *tennis elbow*. But if you like to play video games, then you'll probably get *arcade elbow* or even *video wrist*. Doctors have been warning children about the health dangers of playing video games. Besides sore wrists and elbows, video-game players can get eyestrain and aching feet. Worst of all is a terrible sickness called totally broke.

**4.** People have long wondered what causes disease. Years ago, people felt that illness was a result of demons. Others thought sick people had too much blood. Some felt that disease was a punishment from angry gods. People laughed at the idea that germs caused disease.

**5.** Most tigers don't eat people. Usually they kill people when they are frightened. But some tigers develop a taste for people. The worst man-eating tiger ate more than four hundred people before she was killed. Today people in India are using wired dummies to train tigers not to attack people. When the tigers bite the real-looking dummies, the beasts get a big shock and run away.

_____ **1.** The story mainly tells
- **A.** what kind of pet the poet Virgil had
- **B.** how a fly helped a man keep his property
- **C.** how the government took land
- **D.** how much the pet's funeral cost

_____ **2.** The story mainly tells
- **A.** which grains are used to make puffed cereals
- **B.** how cereal is puffed
- **C.** how hot the ovens are
- **D.** how the grain is removed from the cannons

_____ **3.** The story mainly tells
- **A.** the health dangers of playing video games
- **B.** what video games are best to play
- **C.** why children get eyestrain
- **D.** how people can get tennis elbow

_____ **4.** The story mainly tells
- **A.** why people thought germs couldn't cause illness
- **B.** why people thought demons caused disease
- **C.** about people's ideas on causes of disease long ago
- **D.** why disease was a punishment from the gods

_____ **5.** The story mainly tells
- **A.** about a way of training tigers not to attack people
- **B.** how many people the hungriest tiger in history ate
- **C.** what tigers like to eat
- **D.** how tigers are getting a shock

**1.** Many superstitions seem silly. But a superstition from World War I may be based on truth. This is the belief that lighting three cigarettes from one match is unlucky. At night a match that stayed lit long enough to light three cigarettes could be very unlucky because it could draw enemy fire.

**2.** An odd burst of energy in space puzzled astronomer Jocelyn Bell. Because friends joked about "little green men" sending messages, the burst was named LGM-1. But more signals appeared, and scientists finally found out that stars were exploding and giving off energy. This burst of power that Bell found was called a pulsar.

**3.** You've heard of Paul Revere's ride. But Sybil Ludington, who was 16, made a longer, more courageous ride. In 1777 a rider warned that the British were attacking. Ludington jumped on her horse and went to spread the alarm, riding 40 miles in one night. The American soldiers she alerted drove the British back to their ships.

**4.** A professor examined murder reports in Miami for 15 years. The rate of killings did not stay constant. A chart that noted the dates of the murders and the cycles of the moon was made. The professor found that the murder rate was highest during a full moon.

**5.** The Siamese fighting fish has interesting habits. An angry male fighting fish changes colors. Its scales turn red, green, blue, and purple. The male fighting fish also helps hatch the fish eggs. After the eggs are laid, he gathers them into his mouth and blows them into a nest made of bubbles. He then stays on guard to protect the eggs.

_____ **1.** The story mainly tells

    **A.** how matches stay lit at night

    **B.** why superstitions are silly

    **C.** how soldiers acted during World War I

    **D.** how one superstition may have begun

_____ **2.** The story mainly tells

    **A.** when people thought aliens were sending messages

    **B.** about the discovery of pulsars

    **C.** why exploding stars give off energy

    **D.** how little green men send messages

_____ **3.** The story mainly tells

    **A.** how far Ludington rode in one night

    **B.** who the American soldiers were fighting

    **C.** about Ludington's brave ride

    **D.** what happened to Paul Revere on his ride

_____ **4.** The story mainly tells

    **A.** how people are murdered in Miami, Florida

    **B.** what charts are used for

    **C.** how the moon seems to affect the murder rate

    **D.** how long the professor worked

_____ **5.** The story mainly tells

    **A.** how the male fish helps hatch eggs

    **B.** how the male fish builds a nest

    **C.** why the male fish changes colors

    **D.** what unusual things the fighting fish does

**1.** If you go to Cocos Island near Costa Rica, take a shovel. Three treasures may be hidden there. The first pirate to visit Cocos hid 100 tons of silver. The second pirate hid 150 tons of gold. The third treasure was buried by a ship captain who had stolen 14 tons of gold and many jewels. But no one has ever found these stolen treasures.

**2.** There is a new science called ergonomics. It is the study of the way that offices can be made more comfortable. Scientists are looking at how furniture, light, colors, and machines affect people. If workers get headaches, their office light could be too bright. If workers get tired easily, they might need a more cheerful color of paint on their office walls.

**3.** A man in Germany lives in a treehouse. He trained some trees to grow toward each other. He tied the branches of some trees together and fastened nets on the inside and outside for protection. Then he planted vines to cover the outside. Finally he laid foam blocks down for the floor and put material on the walls for decoration.

**4.** Centuries ago, people believed in creatures called basilisks. According to myth these monsters were created when a rooster laid an egg that was hatched by snakes. This reptile was supposed to be able to kill with its breath or a single look. A person with a mirror could kill a basilisk. The sight of the beast's own image scared it to death.

**5.** Doctors are learning to use imagination in order to cure disease. People may feel helpless when they are sick. It can make them more sick. Today many patients are taught to pretend their white blood cells are knights fighting diseases. They are also told to think of themselves as being completely well. These patients actually get well faster!

_____ **1.** The story mainly tells

    **A.** where Cocos Island is located

    **B.** what you should take if you go to Cocos Island

    **C.** about treasures perhaps hidden on Cocos Island

    **D.** where the third treasure came from

_____ **2.** The story mainly tells

    **A.** what to do when you get a headache or backache

    **B.** why it's good to have plants in the office

    **C.** how offices can be made into better places

    **D.** why machines in people's offices are harmful

_____ **3.** The story mainly tells

    **A.** how a man built a treehouse

    **B.** how to train trees to grow toward each other

    **C.** which materials are for decorating walls

    **D.** which trees make good houses

_____ **4.** The story mainly tells

    **A.** whether or not the basilisk was a real animal

    **B.** how people could hunt deadly basilisks

    **C.** what people once believed about basilisks

    **D.** how basilisks were hatched

_____ **5.** The story mainly tells

    **A.** how helpless people feel when they're sick

    **B.** how doctors use white blood cells

    **C.** how knights fight disease

    **D.** how imagination can help sick people get better

# UNIT 6

1.  Malaria is a serious disease caused by sick mosquitoes. Many Africans were bitten and caught the disease. But some of these people who were bitten stayed well because of changes in the cells of their bodies. These changes protected them from the illness. Over the years this change was passed down to their children.

2.  Many books printed long ago are falling apart. A chemical in the paper causes the paper to crack. Wrapping old books in plastic and freezing them can preserve them. Most libraries use special gases to stop the paper from cracking.

3.  There was an African American woman who couldn't walk from age 4 to age 6. But she became "the fastest woman alive." Two serious illnesses left Wilma Rudolph's legs weak. But her family helped her exercise. She learned to walk again. At 16 she ran in the Olympic games. At 20 she won 3 Olympic gold medals.

4.  There are some odd laws today. Dynamite can't be used in fishing. It would kill all the fish in the lake. Hunting isn't allowed on the streets. Hunters could shoot people by mistake. Debt collectors can't wear costumes. They aren't allowed to scare people by dressing as police officers.

5.  Thomas Dewey ran for President during World War II. He learned that the United States had cracked the Japanese secret code. Dewey wondered "If the President knew that the Japanese would attack Pearl Harbor, why did he let men die?" Dewey knew that if he told about this, he'd win the election. But the enemy would also change their code. So he kept this secret. Records later showed that the President hadn't known about the code.

_____  **1.** The story mainly tells

       **A.** how a change in body cells protected people

       **B.** what malaria is and how it's spread

       **C.** where the change in the genes occurred

       **D.** who is likely to have the change in genes

_____  **2.** The story mainly tells

       **A.** how books can be frozen

       **B.** how old books can be preserved

       **C.** what causes the paper to become brittle

       **D.** how much it costs to preserve a book

_____  **3.** The story mainly tells

       **A.** how Rudolph's family helped her

       **B.** about the age limits of the Olympics

       **C.** how overcoming illness led to 3 gold medals

       **D.** the number of track records set by Rudolph

_____  **4.** The story mainly tells

       **A.** why hunting animals on streets isn't allowed

       **B.** how dynamite can be used to catch fish

       **C.** about some odd laws that are around today

       **D.** how debt collectors must dress

_____  **5.** The story mainly tells

       **A.** how the government knew about Japan's plans

       **B.** why Dewey told the people

       **C.** how Dewey kept a secret

       **D.** how the Japanese attacked Pearl Harbor

**1.** The oldest known living tree is a bristlecone pine found in California. People have named the tree Methuselah because it is so old. By counting its rings, they have determined that this tree is 4,600 years old.

**2.** A pie-throwing contest is held every year in England. People hired to be targets stick their heads through a hole in the middle of a bull's eye. The pie can be any flavor, but it can't be bigger than ten inches across. The throwers earn points according to how well they hit their targets. If they hit the target right in the face, they score six points.

**3.** Try the following experiment. Hold your hand close to a mirror, and you'll see two reflections. One will be very clear, but the other one will be faint, like a shadow. A mirror reflects when light bounces off your hand and goes through the glass to the back of the mirror. Then the light bounces toward your eyes. But sometimes the light gets caught and bounces between the front and back of the mirror before it bounces outward. That's what makes the shadow reflection.

**4.** Most people think that the first houses settlers built in America were log cabins. But the Pilgrims lived in wigwams made of poles, clay, and bark. The first log cabins in America were built by Swedish pioneers, who settled in Delaware 18 years after the Pilgrims arrived.

**5.** Giraffes are the tallest animals. They stand about 17 feet high, but almost 7 feet of that is neck! The giraffe's legs are extremely long, too. The animals can easily step over a fence that is 6 feet high.

_____ **1.** The story mainly tells

   **A.** about the oldest known living tree
   **B.** how to tell a tree's age
   **C.** how old redwood trees are
   **D.** where the bristlecone pine is located

_____ **2.** The story mainly tells

   **A.** how to throw a pie at someone
   **B.** what the job of being a pie target is like
   **C.** how much the biggest pie in England weighed
   **D.** what an English pie-throwing contest is like

_____ **3.** The story mainly tells

   **A.** why you can see two reflections in a mirror
   **B.** why it's unlucky to break a mirror
   **C.** how to see shadows
   **D.** how light bounces off objects

_____ **4.** The story mainly tells

   **A.** how the Pilgrims lived
   **B.** how Swedish pioneers lived underground
   **C.** about the early types of houses built by settlers
   **D.** how to build a log cabin

_____ **5.** The story mainly tells

   **A.** how to run 35 miles an hour
   **B.** what giraffes like to eat
   **C.** how tall giraffes are
   **D.** why animals hunt giraffes

**1.** Historians are trying to solve the mystery of Stonehenge, a monument in England that is made up of a ring of huge stones. Some stones weigh fifty tons and were brought from three hundred miles away! Scientists think that Stonehenge was a place of worship many years ago. Others think that the stones were used to help people predict changes in the sun and moon.

**2.** Researchers studied snack foods to determine which ones caused cavities. Cake, raisins, and bananas caused the most cavities. Chocolate, potato chips, and peanuts weren't quite as bad. Fatty foods coat and protect the teeth, but sticky foods cling. The acids in sticky foods have more time to rot the teeth.

**3.** Lasers are instruments that produce a special kind of light. The light from a laser is very narrow and doesn't spread out the way sunlight does. The beam is powerful because the light is concentrated. Some laser beams cut through steel. Other lasers can be used to send television signals. Doctors use lasers to burn diseased cells, do eye operations, or close wounds. Lasers are new, useful scientific tools.

**4.** Pearls are formed when an oyster swallows a bit of sand. The oyster covers the sand grain with *nacre*, a smooth, shiny substance that keeps the sand from hurting the oyster and grows into a pearl. As the pearl grows, it can become white, black, pink, orange, purple, or gold. From tiny bits of sand, the oyster can grow a pearl that weighs more than 14 pounds and costs more than 32 million dollars!

**5.** A Greek myth tells how a man named Daedalus created wings and flew. Now scientists are building the *Daedalus Project*. They are building an airplane that can be pedaled in the same way as a bicycle. The light plane will have a fifty-foot wingspan. Someday this type of plane might allow astronauts to fly on Mars.

_____ 1. The story mainly tells

    A. where the Stonehenge monument is located

    B. how big the rocks at Stonehenge are

    C. how far some of the Stonehenge rocks were carried

    D. what scientists believe Stonehenge's purpose was

_____ 2. The story mainly tells

    A. why cake causes tooth decay

    B. when sweet foods cause cavities in teeth

    C. why some foods cause more cavities than others

    D. why fatty foods are very likely to cause cavities

_____ 3. The story mainly tells

    A. whether a laser beam is wide or narrow

    B. why a laser's light is so powerful

    C. some of the useful ways to use laser beams

    D. what things can be cut with a laser

_____ 4. The story mainly tells

    A. how pearls are formed

    B. what colors natural pearls may be

    C. what sea animals can create pearls

    D. what the biggest pearl in the world is worth

_____ 5. The story mainly tells

    A. who Daedalus was and what he did

    B. what the Daedalus Project is

    C. how long the Daedalus Project flight will be

    D. how the special plane will be powered

**1.** Dolls are popular toys today, but they had other uses in the past. The Hopis used sacred dolls to teach children about spirits. In ancient Egypt, dolls were sometimes buried with people. These dolls would be servants in the ghost world. In America, pioneer women learned about fashion in England from fancy-dressed dolls.

**2.** Strange winds may cause some people in Europe and North Africa to feel bad. These winds are called siroccos, and they blow near mountains and deserts. Some people get headaches or can't sleep when the winds blow. Other people have accidents or get angry. A chemical in people's bodies increases when the winds blow. Scientists think that this may cause some people to feel sick.

**3.** A new medicine for wounds has been found—sugar! There were some patients sick with skin ulcers. *Skin ulcers* are ugly, open sores that don't heal. A doctor tried sugar and found that it worked. Since then sugar has been used on more than three thousand injuries. French doctors tried the treatment on people who had heart operations and found that the sugared wounds healed much faster than usual.

**4.** People used to dance to cure spider bites. Taranto, an Italian town, had many spiders called tarantulas. People feared these ugly but harmless spiders. They thought that a bite could kill. Fast dancing was supposed to make people sweat and release the spider's poison. A country dance called the tarantella got its start from this belief.

**5.** Scientists have tried teaching chimpanzees how to talk. But chimps can't speak with words. So they are learning the sign language used by people who are deaf. The chimps ask questions and create new words, such as *red drink fruit* for *watermelon.* Some chimps even try to teach sign language to other animals.

 

_____ **1.** The story mainly tells

    **A.** why dolls were sometimes buried

    **B.** which purposes dolls have served

    **C.** which Native American tribe used sacred dolls

    **D.** how people learned about fashion from dolls

_____ **2.** The story mainly tells

    **A.** why some people get sick

    **B.** how certain winds may affect people's health

    **C.** why winds blow near mountains

    **D.** where the strange winds are likely to occur

_____ **3.** The story mainly tells

    **A.** who first thought of using sugar on wounds

    **B.** how sugar can help heal wounds

    **C.** how many people have been treated with sugar

    **D.** how sugar has been used in heart operations

_____ **4.** The story mainly tells

    **A.** which town in Italy had many spiders

    **B.** whether the Italian tarantulas were poisonous

    **C.** why people danced to cure spider bites

    **D.** how country dances were created

_____ **5.** The story mainly tells

    **A.** what kind of monkeys are learning to talk

    **B.** what language the chimps use in the tests

    **C.** how chimps are learning sign language

    **D.** whether other animals can learn special languages

**1.** Imagine cheating in a World Series! In 1919 someone paid eight Chicago White Sox baseball players to lose games in the Series. The people who paid the players bet money that the team would lose the games. The bettors hoped to make much money. The players who cheated were punished severely and were never allowed to play baseball again.

**2.** The peanut is a humble plant with hundreds of functions. Most peanuts are roasted in their shells and lightly salted. About half the peanuts eaten in our country are ground into a thick paste called peanut butter. The rich oil made from peanuts is good for frying foods and is used for oiling machines and making soaps, paint, and explosives. Even peanut shells are used to make plastics and to fertilize soil.

**3.** The lack of gravity in space makes even simple tasks a challenge. Astronauts have to wear boots that hold their feet to the floor so that they can walk around. Eating is a real chore. Dried and frozen foods are stored in plastic bags. To eat chicken soup, the astronauts cut a hole in one end of the bag and squeeze the soup into their mouths.

**4.** "The War of the Worlds," a radio story, once started a panic. Because many people didn't hear that it was just a story about monsters from space, they thought the fake news bulletins were true. People were frantic. It took hours to calm them down and convince them that it was only a radio play.

**5.** Some college teachers in Michigan have made a small computer that looks like an apple. It will be picked and handled like real fruit. Since much fruit is damaged on its way to market, this machine will measure shaking and temperature changes. The computerized apple will help people find ways to avoid damaging fruits during shipping.

_____ **1.** The story mainly tells

    **A.** which city the ball players were from
    **B.** who paid the players
    **C.** why some ball players cheated in a World Series
    **D.** how the guilty players were punished

_____ **2.** The story mainly tells

    **A.** why peanut oil is used for frying
    **B.** how much peanut butter is eaten in our country
    **C.** about the many uses of the peanut
    **D.** why peanut shells make good fertilizer

_____ **3.** The story mainly tells

    **A.** why there is little gravity in space
    **B.** why easy tasks are challenging in space
    **C.** why space food is stored in plastic bags
    **D.** how to eat chicken soup

_____ **4.** The story mainly tells

    **A.** what people thought about news stories
    **B.** why people were afraid of the monsters
    **C.** how a radio play fooled many people
    **D.** where the monsters in the story came from

_____ **5.** The story mainly tells

    **A.** where the computerized apple was created
    **B.** how the computer company helped make the machine
    **C.** what the computerized apple looks like
    **D.** about the purpose of the computerized apple

**1.** Many people in India don't eat beef. Even though Indians don't eat cattle, they still find many uses for cattle. The cows search through and eat the garbage and weeds that people can't use. Cows also provide milk and other milk products. Young cattle are used for plowing fields and carrying big loads.

**2.** There are many ways to learn about people. You can learn much about people by simply watching or talking to them. Looking at the floor can also give you information about people. You can tell where people walk most frequently because of the worn carpet. The next time you're in someone else's car, listen to the radio. The type of music played on the station can tell much about the person. You can discover whether people are dieting by just looking inside their refrigerators.

**3.** The diamond is a hard element that can cut through almost any metal. That is why it is often used for industrial purposes. Whole diamond stones are set into tools. Dust from crushed diamond stones is used for coating the edges of tools. But care must be taken when exposing diamonds to extreme heat because heat can turn them into graphite. Graphite is the soft material used in the manufacture of lead for pencils.

**4.** A scientist believes that millions of animals have died every 26 million years. He thinks that comets are responsible for those deaths. Comets would explode on impact as they slammed into Earth. Dust from the explosions blocked light and heat from the sun. Because plants and animals on Earth could not withstand such conditions, they died.

**5.** Fabergé, a jeweler, made Easter eggs from rare metals and jewels. A Russian emperor liked them so much that he often gave them away as gifts. The elaborate eggs are only a few inches high. Some have tiny clocks inside them. Others hold small pictures or toys. The highest price ever paid for a Fabergé egg was more than one and one-half million dollars!

_____ **1.** The story mainly tells

    **A.** how cows are used in India

    **B.** where some people do not eat beef

    **C.** which cows plow fields

    **D.** what milk is used for

_____ **2.** The story mainly tells

    **A.** how to guess where people walk

    **B.** how to learn about people

    **C.** how to listen to the radio

    **D.** how to watch people

_____ **3.** The story mainly tells

    **A.** how to turn a diamond into graphite

    **B.** how diamonds are used in industry

    **C.** how diamond dust coats tool edges

    **D.** when diamonds are used in pencils

_____ **4.** The story mainly tells

    **A.** how often animals died

    **B.** why comets may come near the earth

    **C.** where the dust comes from

    **D.** about a probable cause of animal deaths in the past

_____ **5.** The story mainly tells

    **A.** what Fabergé eggs are like

    **B.** who bought and gave the eggs as gifts

    **C.** what Fabergé eggs have in them

    **D.** how Fabergé made the eggs

1. Spices were important even in ancient times. They made everyday foods taste better. Doctors told people to eat spices to stay healthy. The strong flavors of the spices hid the taste of spoiled food. Rich people showed off their wealth by using many spices in their cooking.

2. Could you catch a baseball traveling 2 miles a minute? Gabby Street of the Washington Senators did. A friend wondered whether Gabby could catch a baseball dropped from the 555-foot-high Washington Monument. So in 1908 a man dropped 13 balls from the monument. The wind blew almost all of the baseballs out of reach. But Street caught the last one as it plunged.

3. The tulip was very popular in the 1600s. The Dutch bought the bulbs, hoping to make money. One tulip bulb sold for 12 tons of grain, 24 animals, and some fancy clothes. But soon no one would pay high prices for the tulip bulbs. Many people who bought tulips lost all their money. Finally the government had to control the trade in bulbs.

4. Each year experts study the movie habits of Americans. The study shows some interesting facts. For example, did you know that teenagers go to more movies than any other age group? Almost one half of all Americans are over 40. But only 15 of every 100 moviegoers are in this age group. This explains the big success of movies about teenagers.

5. Scientists believed for a long time that a certain kind of fish had been extinct for sixty million years. But in 1938 a living fish of that type was caught near South Africa. Another fish like the first one was caught near the Comoro Islands. The people of the islands had eaten the fish for years. They used the scales of the fish to patch bicycle tires. While scientists thought the fish was rare, the people thought it was ordinary.

_____ **1.** The story mainly tells

    **A.** how food was kept from spoiling

    **B.** how spices were used in ancient times

    **C.** how some people stayed healthy

    **D.** when people used spices a lot

_____ **2.** The story mainly tells

    **A.** where the baseballs were dropped

    **B.** how Street caught a ball traveling 2 miles a minute

    **C.** how fast the baseballs fell

    **D.** what team Street played for

_____ **3.** The story mainly tells

    **A.** what flower was popular in the 1600s

    **B.** how much one bulb sold for

    **C.** where the flower craze took place

    **D.** how the tulip trade became government-controlled

_____ **4.** The story mainly tells

    **A.** about the movie habits of Americans

    **B.** about the movie habits of teenagers

    **C.** why teenagers like movies

    **D.** why the smallest group of moviegoers is over 40

_____ **5.** The story mainly tells

    **A.** about a fish thought to be extinct

    **B.** why a certain kind of fish was extinct

    **C.** how the scales of a fish were used to patch tires

    **D.** how scientists caught a rare type of fish

**1.** The earth's surface is made up of about twenty rigid plates, or sections of earth. These plates move slowly past each other. As they move, the rocks at the edges of the plates are squeezed and pulled apart. When the force of the movement is too great, the rocks shift and shatter, causing an earthquake.

**2.** Rescuers fought to free a man caught in a burning truck. The metal was so badly twisted that even a wrecker couldn't budge it. Then suddenly a stranger ripped a door off the cab with his bare hands, twisted the steering wheel away, and braced his shoulders under the crushed top to lift it. Later, people found out that the stranger had once lost a child in a fire. His hatred of fire apparently gave him the enormous strength to save the trapped man.

**3.** North Carolina police may use germs to catch bank thieves. Important papers can be sprayed with harmless germs that will stick to the hands of anyone who touches the paper. If a dishonest employee steals the papers, things that he or she touches later will have the germs on them. A scientist can show that the person leaving the germs got them when stealing the treated papers.

**4.** Annie Oakley was famous for her shooting ability. She learned to shoot when she was only 8 and won a shooting match against a great marksperson at 15. For many years she performed in Buffalo Bill's Wild West Show. Once when she was in England, the Prince of Wales gave Oakley a silver cup. On it was written, "You are the best shot I have ever seen."

**5.** A French company found that people can make food out of oil. Fertilizers are added to the oil. Oxygen is then pumped through the liquid. This mixture encourages the growth of high-protein yeasts. The tasteless, odorless yeasts are used to feed starving people.

_____  **1.** The story mainly tells

    **A.** what makes up the earth's surface

    **B.** how the plates form a surface

    **C.** how plate movement causes an earthquake

    **D.** how plates move

_____  **2.** The story mainly tells

    **A.** how a man got caught in a fire

    **B.** how to get someone out of a wrecked truck

    **C.** how strong the stranger was

    **D.** how a man's emotions helped him save a life

_____  **3.** The story mainly tells

    **A.** how some germs are harmless to people

    **B.** when crooked bank employees steal important things

    **C.** how police use germs to solve crimes

    **D.** how important papers are treated

_____  **4.** The story mainly tells

    **A.** when Buffalo Bill's Wild West Show performed

    **B.** how Oakley was a famous marksperson

    **C.** when the Prince of Wales gave Oakley a cup

    **D.** how Frank Butler met Oakley

_____  **5.** The story mainly tells

    **A.** how oil becomes food for starving people

    **B.** which fertilizers are added to the mixture

    **C.** what the yeasts taste and smell like

    **D.** which people are fed this food

**1.** Imagine buying groceries with piles of money! Germany had economic problems after World War I. Among them was a terrible money problem. The government printed much money, and almost everyone had plenty of cash. But everything was very expensive because the cash was almost worthless. A sack of bills might buy one loaf of bread. One woman left a laundry basket of cash alone for a minute. While she was gone, a thief stole the basket but left the money!

**2.** If you were invited to dinner during the Middle Ages, you would have to be certain to wash your hands. At that time people had only spoons and their fingers to eat with, and they shared plates. Scratching an itch at the table was very impolite because you might carry the flea that was biting you to the common food dish. But after dinner you would throw the bones on the floor for the dogs!

**3.** Although Albert Einstein was one of the greatest scientists of all time, he failed almost all his classes in high school. Thomas Edison, the inventor, attended school for only three months. Harriet Tubman was a slave with no formal schooling. But she used her knowledge of the forest to help more than three hundred people escape from slavery!

**4.** According to a myth, the gods granted King Midas one wish. The greedy king wished that everything he touched would turn to gold. He enjoyed making his palace gold. But he soon cursed the gift because when he tried to eat, the food became gold. Midas asked the gods to remove his golden touch, and the gods answered his prayer.

**5.** Bamboo is a giant grass. It grows very fast. One type of bamboo grows 3 feet in 24 hours! The bamboo is hollow and light but very strong. Bamboo is so strong that it can be made into fences, roofs, boats, and furniture. However, young bamboo is tender, and people eat its beautiful, green shoots.

_____  **1.** The story mainly tells

    **A.** about Germany's money problem after the war

    **B.** what a thief stole

    **C.** how much money people in Germany had

    **D.** how the government printed money

_____  **2.** The story mainly tells

    **A.** what table manners were like in the Middle Ages

    **B.** where people threw bones after dinner

    **C.** why scratching at dinner was bad manners

    **D.** why people ate with spoons

_____  **3.** The story mainly tells

    **A.** why Albert Einstein failed classes

    **B.** how people did great things without schooling

    **C.** why Thomas Edison was taught at home

    **D.** how Harriet Tubman used her knowledge

_____  **4.** The story mainly tells

    **A.** why Midas earned a wish

    **B.** what Midas's wish was

    **C.** how Midas's wish was really a mistake

    **D.** how the gods answered Midas's request

_____  **5.** The story mainly tells

    **A.** how fast bamboo can grow

    **B.** what the bamboo looks like

    **C.** how people eat bamboo plants

    **D.** how useful the bamboo plant is

**1.** A clerk made a two-million-dollar mistake because of a comma. He was supposed to write, "All foreign fruit plants are duty-free." It allowed growers to import fruit trees without paying taxes. Instead, he wrote, "All foreign fruit, plants are duty-free." Because of the comma, fruits and plants were imported free of tax. It cost the country two million dollars.

**2.** "Gold! I see gold!" Howard Carter exclaimed. He was an archaeologist and had just opened King Tut's tomb. Inside he saw golden chairs, jeweled necklaces, and battle trumpets that had been silent for thousands of years. King Tut's mummy was found inside a solid gold case that was more than six feet long!

**3.** People used to play football bareheaded. After many injuries, players began to use plain, leather caps. Plastic helmets and masks appeared later. Still, many players were getting hurt. To make the helmets better, designers studied—woodpeckers! Their tough, spongy skulls became the model for modern football helmets.

**4.** During the Civil War, Mary Ann Bickerdyke organized Union Army hospitals. She fought to get food and clothing for the sick soldiers. At one time she found a doctor wearing a shirt and shoes that were intended for patients. Bickerdyke pushed him down and pulled off the clothes. The soldiers cheered and laughed. The embarrassed doctor transferred to another hospital.

**5.** Light-colored trees grew in England. On these trees rested light-colored moths. Since the moths were the same color as the trees, birds could not see the insects and eat them. Then cities grew older. Dirty air turned the trees in the cities a dark color. Birds could then see the light-colored moths and eat them. After many years the moths were born a dark color. They could hide on the dirty trees, lay their eggs, hatch their young, and survive in the modern world.

_____ **1.** The story mainly tells

    **A.** how much money was lost

    **B.** about a very expensive error

    **C.** why fruit and plants should be taxed

    **D.** how people pay taxes when they import items

_____ **2.** The story mainly tells

    **A.** what Howard Carter did for a living

    **B.** about the archaeological discovery of the king's tomb

    **C.** where the king's mummy was found

    **D.** what the mummy case was made of

_____ **3.** The story mainly tells

    **A.** why football helmets must be strong and light

    **B.** when leather caps were used in football

    **C.** about the role of the woodpecker in helmet design

    **D.** why many players are injured

_____ **4.** The story mainly tells

    **A.** why Bickerdyke helped the Union Army

    **B.** why the doctor was so embarrassed

    **C.** how Bickerdyke embarrassed a doctor

    **D.** what items the doctor had stolen from patients

_____ **5.** The story mainly tells

    **A.** how moths adapted to their surroundings

    **B.** how birds find moths on trees

    **C.** the color of trees in cities

    **D.** how cities grew

**1.** Potatoes were a big crop in Ireland. People raised grain and cows to sell, but they lived off their potatoes. Suddenly in 1845 the potato plants died. More than seven hundred thousand people starved to death. Others moved to America, seeking a better life.

**2.** A scientist took some baby monkeys from their mothers. Each baby monkey was put in a cage by itself. The scientist gave each monkey a doll that looked like its mother, but they were not allowed to see others of their own kind. When the monkeys were grown, they were put in cages with other monkeys. But they didn't like the other monkeys, and some even rejected their own babies.

**3.** Corn was first grown by Native Americans. They showed the Pilgrims how to grow it as food. At one time corn was used as money by the pioneers. Corn is used as feed for farm animals. People eat it as a vegetable. Oil, starch, and sugar can be made from corn. Corn is also important in industry. Medicine, paper, fertilizer, and glue can be made from corn and corn products.

**4.** Atom bombs landed on two Japanese cities during World War II. Many people died in the explosions and fires. Later, people in the bombed cities felt weak and tired. They lost their hair and developed big bruises. Women in the area often gave birth to dead babies. Years later, people were still dying from cancer.

**5.** The young Pony Express riders often had to ride their horses through rivers. The weather was usually hot and dry. The riders were often afraid because they had to pass through dangerous country. They usually traveled 75 miles a day. The riders were paid about 100 dollars a month for their work.

_____ **1.** The story mainly tells

        **A.** when potatoes were an important food
           for the Irish

        **B.** what happened when the Irish potato crop failed

        **C.** how many people starved

        **D.** when people came to America

_____ **2.** The story mainly tells

        **A.** how being raised alone affected some monkeys

        **B.** how monkeys act

        **C.** what kinds of cages monkeys lived in

        **D.** how some monkeys ignored their babies

_____ **3.** The story mainly tells

        **A.** what kinds of animals eat corn

        **B.** about the importance of corn

        **C.** who first grew corn for food

        **D.** who used corn instead of money

_____ **4.** The story mainly tells

        **A.** how bombs caused explosions

        **B.** when people died from cancer

        **C.** some of the effects of the atom bombs on Japan

        **D.** what happened in World War II

_____ **5.** The story mainly tells

        **A.** how far Pony Express riders rode in a day

        **B.** about the demanding job of a Pony Express rider

        **C.** how much money a Pony Express rider made

        **D.** what the weather was like

**1.** Liu Shih-kun was a skilled musician. In the 1960s the Chinese government disliked his piano music, but Shih-kun refused to play the music it wanted him to play. He spent more than seven years in jail. Although he couldn't play his piano there, he could practice playing it in his mind. After he was released, he played just as well as before.

**2.** CAT scanners are used by doctors, not vets. The scanner is an x-ray machine that photographs soft tissue. A special dye is injected into a person. The machine then takes many photos. A computer combines these to show the person's organs, which the doctors then examine. The CAT scanner lessens the need for operations.

**3.** Before printing was invented, people wrote each book by hand. They decorated the pages with pictures. Sometimes people wrote books in silver and gold ink. Because the books were so expensive, only the rich could buy them. In the 1300s a Bible cost enough money to pay an average worker for 26 years.

**4.** At one time many babies died from bad milk. Milk companies knew that germs could be killed by heating the milk. But they didn't believe it was necessary. Then Nathan Straus went into the business of selling milk. But he went to the trouble of heating the milk very carefully. His customers didn't get sick. Health officials realized that boiling the milk was important. Soon it was required that all milk sold had to be heated. The disease rate dropped.

**5.** Ancient Roman emperors tried making people happy by giving grain away. It was supposed to relieve poverty. But people insisted that free food was a basic right. At one time one out of three people received free wheat. The government nearly ran out of money. It gave away grain, meat, and oil.

_____ **1.** The story mainly tells

    **A.** how long Shih-kun stayed in prison

    **B.** how mental practice helped Shih-kun's musical skills

    **C.** why the Chinese government didn't like music

    **D.** what kind of instrument Shih-kun played

_____ **2.** The story mainly tells

    **A.** who uses a CAT scanner

    **B.** what *CAT* stands for

    **C.** how the CAT scanner helps doctors

    **D.** what kind of computer is used

_____ **3.** The story mainly tells

    **A.** how much a Bible cost long ago

    **B.** how printing was invented

    **C.** how valuable books were long ago

    **D.** how books were written in gold

_____ **4.** The story mainly tells

    **A.** how to kill disease germs in milk

    **B.** how Straus changed the milk business

    **C.** why companies charged so much for their milk

    **D.** why Straus was a generous man

_____ **5.** The story mainly tells

    **A.** how emperors gave food away

    **B.** when people received free food

    **C.** how the Roman food program failed

    **D.** which Roman emperors were charitable

**1.** Because wood was needed for ships, many trees from Greek forests were cut down. At first the local farmers were happy. There was more cleared land for planting. But rain began washing away the good topsoil. Later, people cut down shallow-rooted trees to make room for valuable olive trees. More erosion occurred, and large sections of Greece became barren.

**2.** A store was selling pairs of blue jeans that were stained. Many people bought the jeans. Some people wore the stained jeans right away. Others washed them before wearing them. The people who didn't wash their jeans first got sick. But those people who washed them stayed well. Later, doctors found out that the stains on the jeans were poisonous.

**3.** John Sager's family was on its way to Oregon, when his parents suddenly died. But Sager and his six brothers and sisters decided that they would keep traveling. Knowing that some adults would object, the children secretly went away on foot. They walked five hundred miles over plains and snow-covered mountains. The weather was bad, and one sister broke a leg. But they continued until they finally reached Oregon.

**4.** In ancient times, people used string to calculate measurements for the great pyramids. Two hundred years ago, people made chairs with wooden pegs instead of with nails. They also made door hinges from leather. Today builders still use string with a weight on one end to make sure that bricks are straight.

**5.** In 1943 the Nazis planned to capture the Jewish people of Warsaw, Poland. To escape the Nazis, the Jewish people smuggled in rifles and built bombs. With these weapons they faced the Nazi soldiers, who were armed with tanks and machine guns. After 28 days of war, the Jewish people lost their desperate fight.

_____ **1.** The story mainly tells

    **A.** what was made with the trees

    **B.** that cutting down trees led to erosion

    **C.** why the Greek farmers were happy at first

    **D.** what kind of tree was considered valuable

_____ **2.** The story mainly tells

    **A.** which people got sick

    **B.** how washing removed the poison from jeans

    **C.** about goods that a store was selling

    **D.** what doctors think about jeans

_____ **3.** The story mainly tells

    **A.** about a dangerous trip made by some children

    **B.** why adults didn't want the children to go

    **C.** why Sager was responsible for the others

    **D.** how some of the children got sick during the trip

_____ **4.** The story mainly tells

    **A.** how string is used

    **B.** how people measured the pyramids

    **C.** how simple objects are useful in construction

    **D.** how door hinges are made from leather

_____ **5.** The story mainly tells

    **A.** when rifles and bombs are used for fighting tanks

    **B.** how long the people fought

    **C.** that the Jewish people didn't surrender easily

    **D.** why the Nazis wanted to capture the Jewish people

**1.** Computers have changed quite a bit through the years. An early model could add eighteen million numbers an hour. One person would have needed many years to do the same job. A modern computer recently added one and one-half trillion numbers. It took only three hours to do it!

**2.** The beaver's front teeth have a hard, bright-orange covering. These teeth are used to cut and tear the bark off trees. The back teeth are flat and rough and are used for chewing. There are two flaps of skin between the front and back teeth. These flaps keep water and splinters from entering the beaver's mouth.

**3.** In 1944 a magazine printed a story about the very powerful atom bomb. The descriptions in the magazine were quite close to the truth about the bomb. The FBI thought this top-secret information had been stolen, but the author had read the details in public records.

**4.** Some Puritans hated their homeland, England. The king would not let them practice their religion as they pleased. They decided to sail to America, which the English had begun to settle. In America they made some strict laws. Everybody had to be a Puritan or leave. Quakers were whipped in public, and priests were hanged. People did not enjoy freedom of religion until 1791.

**5.** Product codes on items consist of bars and numbers on the product label. The first numbers tell which company made the item. The last numbers identify the product and size. A laser reads the bars at the checkout. A computer finds the price for that product and prints the price on the cash-register slip. Store owners can change prices of items by changing the computer. The records in the computer help the owners learn which goods sell well.

_____ **1.** The story mainly tells

    **A.** who uses computers

    **B.** how long one person takes to do a job

    **C.** how computers have gotten faster over time

    **D.** how fast modern computers can add

_____ **2.** The story mainly tells

    **A.** about the color of the front teeth

    **B.** how the two flaps of skin are used

    **C.** about the specially designed mouth of the beaver

    **D.** how splinters get into the beaver's mouth

_____ **3.** The story mainly tells

    **A.** how someone worked on a bomb

    **B.** what FBI agents thought about magazines

    **C.** how the FBI drew the wrong conclusion

    **D.** why a magazine described the bomb

_____ **4.** The story mainly tells

    **A.** why some people were whipped

    **B.** why the Puritans hated England

    **C.** how the Puritans continued an injustice

    **D.** how the king felt about the Puritans of England

_____ **5.** The story mainly tells

    **A.** how the product codes are developed

    **B.** how the product code system is effective

    **C.** how one machine reads the numbers and bars

    **D.** how the numbers are assigned to companies

1. A Cherokee named Sequoya developed an alphabet for his people. The work took 12 years. He made symbols for the 85 different sounds in the language. Soon people learned the new language. Books and papers were printed in Cherokee. The Cherokee people could record the history of their ancient culture and share their knowledge with other people.

2. Insects were ruining Australian sugarcane. A toad was imported from South America to eat the bugs. The three-pound toad ate the sugarcane insects. It then ate crops, other toads, and even helpful bugs. Dogs, cats, and cattle got sick when they tried eating the poisonous toads. The toads also multiplied quickly. Officials offered thirty dollars for each toad—dead or alive.

3. Shock may occur after a bad accident, heart attack, or poisoning. A person in shock is pale and cold. The heartbeat is weak, and the breathing is fast. What can you do if someone is in shock? Call a doctor. Keep the victim warm and quiet until the doctor arrives. Don't try to move the sick person. Shock can kill a person who has even minor injuries.

4. A Dutch artist once painted pictures and signed them with the names of famous artists. Some of these pictures were sold to Nazi officers. After World War II, the artist was arrested for selling art treasures to the enemy. People didn't believe the pictures he sold were fakes. The Dutch artist had to paint a picture in jail before they believed him.

5. Saffron comes from the crocus plant and costs about two thousand dollars a pound! More than seventy thousand crocuses must be picked by hand to get one pound of saffron. In the Middle Ages, people who grew and sold saffron became very rich. Saffron was so valuable that smuggling crocus bulbs was punishable by death!

_____ **1.** The story mainly tells

    **A.** how long Sequoya worked on his alphabet

    **B.** how many symbols the Cherokee language has

    **C.** how Cherokee became a written language

    **D.** how many books were printed in Cherokee

_____ **2.** The story mainly tells

    **A.** how helpful the South American toad was

    **B.** how a bad situation was made even worse

    **C.** how many animals were poisoned

    **D.** how much the toads were worth to officials

_____ **3.** The story mainly tells

    **A.** how to recognize and treat shock

    **B.** when shock is likely to occur

    **C.** what can happen to a person in shock

    **D.** how to treat all accident victims

_____ **4.** The story mainly tells

    **A.** why the artist was arrested after the war

    **B.** how a greedy artist got into trouble

    **C.** who bought the fake pictures from the artist

    **D.** how the artist proved he had painted the pictures

_____ **5.** The story mainly tells

    **A.** why crocus smuggling was punishable by death

    **B.** how expensive saffron has always been

    **C.** how much saffron costs today

    **D.** when people grew very rich

**1.** Native Americans dried strips of meat, pounded it into a paste, and then mixed it with fat. Sometimes they added berries and sugar. Then they pressed it into small cakes. *Pemmican* didn't spoil, and it provided lots of energy for people traveling or going to war. Today explorers still carry and eat this food.

**2.** Because lambs are sometimes eaten by coyotes, ranchers may hunt or trap the coyotes. But killing coyotes may upset nature's balance. Scientists have found a way to protect sheep without killing coyotes. Coyotes are fed lamb meat treated with a drug. When they eat the meat, they get sick. Later, coyotes won't even go near lambs. They'll hunt rabbits instead.

**3.** For years food chemists have tasted hot peppers for chili sauce, catsup, and pizza. But people had a hard time figuring out the spiciness of the peppers. After eating two or three, their taste buds were burning. Now a machine can test different kinds of hot peppers. It measures the chemicals that provide the spicy taste of the peppers.

**4.** The spots on a fawn's coat let it hide in shady areas without being seen. The Viceroy butterfly looks like the bad-tasting Monarch, so birds avoid both. The hognose snake hisses and rolls on its back when it fears another animal. When the opposum is attacked, it plays dead. Distressed turtles hide in their shells until they're sure it's safe to come out again.

**5.** The temperature in Antarctica once fell to 128 degrees below zero Fahrenheit. In the summertime, temperatures average well below freezing. Most of the land is covered with ice that is up to 2 miles thick. Only a few strong mosses and sturdy spiders can live on this big block of ice. Since very little snow or rain falls there, Antarctica is a desert.

**1.** The story mainly tells
   A. who uses pemmican today
   B. what can be put into pemmican
   C. how pemmican was prepared by
      Native Americans
   D. why people eat pemmican today

**2.** The story mainly tells
   A. why coyotes prefer rabbits to lambs
   B. why killing coyotes upsets nature's balance
   C. how scientists protect sheep and coyotes
   D. what kind of people do not like coyotes

**3.** The story mainly tells
   A. how scientists measure chemicals
   B. how hot and spicy peppers are used
   C. why people have trouble tasting hot peppers
   D. how a machine helps the hot-pepper industry

**4.** The story mainly tells
   A. how some animals protect themselves
   B. why some harmless animals look dangerous
   C. why spots or stripes make animals less visible
   D. why birds don't like Monarch butterflies

**5.** The story mainly tells
   A. about a desert with extremely cold temperatures
   B. which plants and insects live in Antarctica
   C. how much snow and rain fall there
   D. how low the temperature once fell

1. Gold has many uses. It has been used as money, in jewelry, and as ornaments. Dentists use gold to fill teeth. Gold can be so finely hammered that light shines through it. The gold used in office windows reduces the drain on the air conditioning.

2. Many American soldiers who die at war are never identified. To honor these unknown soldiers, a tomb was built in Virginia. A few of these soldiers were buried there. They represent all the soldiers who are never identified. The Tomb of the Unknown Soldier is guarded 24 hours a day. It is an honor to be a guard at this monument.

3. In 1815 Mount Tambora blew its top. The huge blast cut four thousand feet off its peak, and it killed twelve thousand people. The dust from the explosion spread around the world. It blocked the sunlight. Europe and America were very cold the following year. In June ten inches of snow fell in New England. The year 1816 was called the year without summer.

4. One hundred viruses placed side by side would be no wider than a human hair. But these germs cause more than 50 diseases. Chicken pox, colds, and rabies are all caused by viruses. More than 21 million people have died from the flu caused by these germs. Scientists are seeking ways to get rid of these tiny killers.

5. Stevie Wonder once said, "A letter puts me on a one-to-one relationship with its sender." He thinks the telephone keeps people from communicating. He blames the distance and the wires for keeping people apart. Wonder thinks that letters are a private form of expression. "It's all very direct and intense," he said. "The letters that move me most are the ones that are honest."

_____ **1.** The story mainly tells
    **A.** why gold is used in jewelry
    **B.** how useful gold is
    **C.** how gold is hammered
    **D.** how office buildings have gold windows

_____ **2.** The story mainly tells
    **A.** why the soldiers could not be identified
    **B.** where the Tomb of the Unknown Soldier is located
    **C.** why the Tomb is guarded all the time
    **D.** why the Tomb of the Unknown Soldier was created

_____ **3.** The story mainly tells
    **A.** how many people died because of Mount Tambora
    **B.** about the effects of a volcanic explosion
    **C.** about the name people gave to the year 1816
    **D.** how much snow fell in New England in June

_____ **4.** The story mainly tells
    **A.** how viruses can be deadly and cause disease
    **B.** how many people died from flu
    **C.** how chicken pox is caused
    **D.** how many people have died from viruses

_____ **5.** The story mainly tells
    **A.** how Wonder writes honest letters
    **B.** when letters are private
    **C.** how telephones help people communicate
    **D.** why Wonder prefers letters to the telephone

**1.** In real life, rattlesnakes try to avoid people and seldom attack. Most people are bitten only after they step on these snakes. A rattlesnake may not even inject its poison when it bites. In fact, more Americans die from insect stings than from snakebites!

**2.** Air plants, such as mosses and lichens, grow on buildings and stones and get their food and water from the air around them. Other plants such as mistletoe get their food and water from the trees they live on. Sometimes these trees die if the plants take away too much food or water.

**3.** Alfred Nobel invented dynamite to help builders. But it was used for war, which made him feel very guilty about the misuse of his invention. He was a rich man, so he set up a nine-million-dollar fund. Today the fund is used to reward people who have improved human life. Nobel Prizes are awarded in six fields, including peace, medicine, and chemistry.

**4.** The rare Chinese panda lives on tender, young bamboo shoots. But most bamboo plants die right after flowering. Without the bamboo the pandas starve. Because some people fear that the rare pandas may die out, in some places food is given to the hungry animals. Some pandas are airlifted to places where bamboo is still plentiful.

**5.** Bob Geldof talked to the top musical talents of the world and asked them to sing at a concert to raise money. The stars agreed. So Geldof found a stadium, arranged for TV coverage, and set up a trust fund. He said that none of the stars would get special treatment. Everyone would work together. In 1985 the Live Aid concert raised more than one hundred million dollars for starving children.

_____  **1.** The story mainly tells
- **A.** when rattlesnakes use their poison
- **B.** why insects kill people
- **C.** how rattlesnakes aren't as dangerous as everyone believes
- **D.** how snakes bite

_____  **2.** The story mainly tells
- **A.** what kinds of plants grow on buildings
- **B.** why mistletoe sometimes kills trees
- **C.** how some plants don't live in soil
- **D.** how mosses and lichens get food and water

_____  **3.** The story mainly tells
- **A.** what the Nobel Prizes are awarded for
- **B.** why Nobel founded the Nobel Prize fund
- **C.** how much money was set aside for rewards
- **D.** what invention Alfred Nobel created

_____  **4.** The story mainly tells
- **A.** what the Chinese pandas usually eat
- **B.** how the bamboo plants flower
- **C.** how people are keeping pandas alive
- **D.** why pandas sometimes starve to death

_____  **5.** The story mainly tells
- **A.** how Geldof found a stadium
- **B.** how many musical stars agreed to sing
- **C.** why people are hungry in Africa
- **D.** how a concert benefited starving children

**1.** Bored by housework, Kitty O'Neil wanted to become a stunt person. Today she performs incredible stunts, such as one-hundred-foot falls. O'Neil has been deaf since birth. But she says she can concentrate better than most hearing people. She is not bothered by the sounds around her.

**2.** Some scientists have been giving the brains of animals small, painless electric shocks. Some beasts fall asleep, while others get angry or scared. An enraged bull whose brain is shocked may suddenly stop while he is charging. These tests help us find out which parts of the brain control different types of behavior.

**3.** Every year hungry deer do millions of dollars' worth of damage to young pine trees. But scientists in Washington have found a way to protect the trees. They use a substance called selenium. Selenium produces a bad smell when dissolved. A bit of this element is put in the ground near trees. Rain dissolves the selenium, and the tree absorbs it. The bad smell keeps the deer away until the tree is fully grown.

**4.** Edith Cavell saved many lives during World War I. She was in charge of a hospital in Belgium. American and British soldiers hid at her hospital. She helped about two hundred of them escape from their enemies. Later she was shot for her brave actions. Her last words were, "Patriotism is not enough." A mountain in Canada is named in Edith Cavell's honor.

**5.** Sharks have a keen sense of hearing and can smell blood from almost two thousand yards away. Sharks also have a special system of channels in their skin that helps them feel the vibrations of a struggling swimmer. We know that in clear water, sharks can see dinner from about fifty feet away. So if you ever spot a shark, always swim away smoothly!

_____ **1.** The story mainly tells

    **A.** when O'Neil fell one hundred feet

    **B.** how long O'Neil has been deaf

    **C.** how O'Neil's disability has helped her career

    **D.** how to become a stunt person

_____ **2.** The story mainly tells

    **A.** what kinds of animals are studied by scientists

    **B.** why an angry bull charges

    **C.** how scientists can change the behavior of animals

    **D.** which parts of the brain control behavior

_____ **3.** The story mainly tells

    **A.** how much damage deer do to trees

    **B.** how trees can be protected from deer

    **C.** what selenium is

    **D.** why deer eat pine trees

_____ **4.** The story mainly tells

    **A.** how Cavell became a hero

    **B.** what kind of work Cavell did for a living

    **C.** what kind of soldiers Cavell helped escape

    **D.** where a mountain is named after Cavell

_____ **5.** The story mainly tells

    **A.** how well sharks hear

    **B.** why sharks have poor vision

    **C.** how sharks sense food

    **D.** when to swim away smoothly

**1.** In colonial times women were printers, whalers, and blacksmiths. Today women are fighting hard to get some of these jobs. For years men didn't deliver babies, but now there are many male doctors. Women's work used to be sewing, cooking, and raising children. But in 1960 the first female prime minister in the world was elected.

**2.** The Masai of East Africa raise cattle for a living. Very little grain is raised in the area, so the people depend on the cattle for food. Most people drink a gallon of milk a day, and beef is a popular meat. Cow's blood is also used as food. It doesn't spoil, it provides protein and minerals, and it can be taken from cows while traveling.

**3.** Allied soldiers in World War II were trapped at Dunkirk, France. They couldn't escape. The shallow water kept rescue ships from landing. But hundreds of people in England took rowboats, tugs, and barges across the English Channel. For eight days this odd navy carried soldiers from the beaches to the large ships. More than three hundred thousand soldiers were taken to safety.

**4.** Plant experts in Bolivia have found some odd potato plants. The potato leaves make a sticky glue. Insects that walk on the plant get caught and starve. Scientists want to breed more potatoes with these sticky leaves. Farmers would be able to grow potatoes and not have to spray their plants with chemicals to get rid of insects.

**5.** Aluminum used to be a very expensive metal. It cost more than five hundred dollars a pound. But in 1886 two scientists dicovered a way to make the metal more cheaply. Two years later another scientist refined the process even more. Then the price of the metal was less than thirty cents a pound. Today aluminum is so cheap that it is often thrown away.

_____ **1.** The story mainly tells

    **A.** how men's and women's jobs have changed

    **B.** how women fought for work

    **C.** why many men are now doctors

    **D.** when the first prime minister was elected

_____ **2.** The story mainly tells

    **A.** how much grain is raised in the world

    **B.** which odd foods people eat in different areas

    **C.** how cows provide food for the Masai

    **D.** what kind of cattle the Masai raise

_____ **3.** The story mainly tells

    **A.** why small ships are better than big ships

    **B.** how many soldiers were saved

    **C.** how soldiers were rescued from Dunkirk

    **D.** why the big ships couldn't get into shallow water

_____ **4.** The story mainly tells

    **A.** how insects are caught by the plants

    **B.** where the special potato plants grow

    **C.** how a special potato plant may help farmers

    **D.** why chemicals are used to kill bugs

_____ **5.** The story mainly tells

    **A.** how much aluminum used to cost

    **B.** how the price of aluminum has changed

    **C.** how scientists refined a process

    **D.** what makes aluminum strong

# *Think and Apply*

## *Building Up to the Main Idea*

Below is a list of different trips. You are packing for each trip.
Write three things you would take along on each trip. Each of
these things is a detail. Each trip is a main idea.

**A.** On a trip to another planet, I would take

1. _____

2. _____

3. _____

**B.** On a camping trip to the mountains, I would take

1. _____

2. _____

3. _____

**C.** On a canoe trip, I would take

1. _____

2. _____

3. _____

**D.** On a trip around the world, I would take

1. _____

2. _____

3. _____

**E.** On an ocean trip, I would take

1. _____

2. _____

3. _____

## *What Kind of Person Are You?*

You can use the main idea to describe your personality. Write the details of the way you treat other people. Then add up those details. What is the main idea? That is what you are like.

**Details**

**1.** The way I treat family members:

_____

_____

_____

**2.** The way I treat teachers:

_____

_____

_____

**3.** The way I treat friends:

_____

_____

_____

**4.** The way I treat neighbors:

_____

_____

_____

**Main Idea**

What I am like:

_____

_____

_____

## Who's There?

You have a visitor knocking at your door. Just by looking, you can tell what the visitor wants. You can figure this out by using details. What the visitor wants is the main idea.

Read each group of details below and then write a main idea for each group.

**1.** *Details:* You see someone in a uniform. He has a mask over his nose and mouth. He's carrying a large canister with a spray nozzle. His van is parked at the curb. The van is white with a large insect painted on the side.

*Main Idea:* This person wants to _____.

**2.** *Details:* You see someone wearing overalls. She has a plunger and a mechanical snake in one hand. In the other hand, she has a tool kit.

*Main Idea:* This person wants to _____.

**3.** *Details:* You see three people who have backed their large van into your driveway. One person is pushing a dolly. The other two people are carrying empty boxes and tape.

*Main Idea:* These people want to_____.

**4.** *Details:* You see someone in a bathing suit. He is holding a towel, suntan lotion, and an inner tube.

*Main Idea:* This person wants to _____.

**To check your answers, turn to page 62.**